INSTAGRAM MARKETING 2019

———— ❧❧❦❧ ————

How to Become a Master Influencer & Influence Millions of Followers Using Highly Effective Personal Branding & Digital Networking Strategies

Gary Loomer

Your Free Gift

As a way of saying thank you for your purchase, I wanted to offer you a free bonus e-book called **10 Easy Ways To Make $2k A Month Passively**

Download the free ebook here: https://www.subscribepage.com/business2k

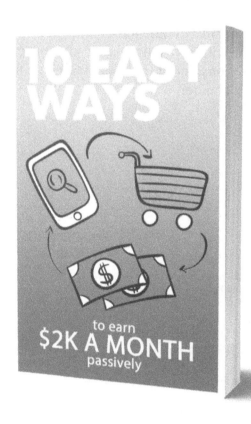

What is passive income and how can it help you to quit your day job. Imagine going to sleep at night, and knowing that your bank accounts are filling up.

In this free guide, you'll discover what passive income and 10 lucrative strategies to earn $2k a month and more.

Listen to this book for free

Do you want to be able to listen to this book whenever you want? Maybe whilst driving to work or running errands. It can be difficult nowadays to sit down and listen to a book. So I am really excited to let you know that this book is available in audio format. What's great is you can get this book for FREE as part of a 30-day audible trial. Thereafter if you don't want to stay an Audible member you can cancel, but keep the book.

Benefits of signing up to audible:

- After the trial, you get 1 free audiobook and 2 free audio originals each month
- Can roll over any unused credits
- Choose from over 425,000 + titles
- Listen anywhere with the Audible app and across multiple devices
- Keep your audiobooks forever, even if you cancel your membership

Click below to get started

Audible US - https://tinyurl.com/yxnvgqne

Audible UK - https://tinyurl.com/yy2oz6pp

Audible FR - https://tinyurl.com/yxc9x457

Audible DE - https://tinyurl.com/yxcpqgsq

TABLE OF CONTENTS

INTRODUCTION

Social media has revolutionized how we communicate with one another. Whether you are an individual messaging an old friend or a multinational company trying to engage millions of customers, social media is the conduit through which true, lasting connections are made. These connections are forged through the stories we tell each other - the ideas, the products, the messages we convey. Of all the social media platforms in existence, it is Instagram which both values and fulfils the potential of storytelling. Marketers have known for decades that the power to build an audience, engage with it, and convert a potential customer into a paying one, is best leveraged through such stories, but it is only now with the advent of social media that this form of communication has been democratized for all.

You hold in your hand the guide to Instagram Marketing in 2019 and beyond. If you are a freelancer hoping to reach new clients, an entrepreneur looking to generate interest in a new business, a large corporation expanding your marketing scope, or an individual needing to engage with the general public - Instagram Marketing 2019 will make these goals a reality.

In each chapter, we will take you step by step through the most cutting-edge and innovative approaches to Instagram marketing. Both new techniques and tried and tested knowledge will be combined to give you the power to not only reach, but surpass your marketing goals. Each chapter contains a brief introduction of what will be covered for easy reference use and will end with a list of learning outcomes, so you can be certain you have picked up everything you need.

Instagram Marketing 2019 is broken down into four parts:

- **Building a Foundation**: An overview of Instagram best practices.

- **Beyond the Basics**: More advanced marketing techniques on Instagram, ensuring you rise above the competition.

- **Monetizing & Marketing**: Ways to leverage your Instagram following in order to create revenue streams.

- **Be Inspired**: Case studies and other inspiring advice from Instagram stars who have already achieved their goals on the platform.

Let us now go on a journey together, so that you can fully realize your marketing potential through Instagram so that you can get your story out there into the world.

PART 1: BUILDING A FOUNDATION

CHAPTER 1: SETTING UP AN EFFECTIVE INSTAGRAM ACCOUNT

In this chapter, we are going to go through the best practices for setting up an effective Instagram account. If you are a seasoned veteran of Instagram, you should still pay close attention to this chapter, as it may help you identify where you have been going wrong and right.

Preparation is King

An Instagram account has a life of its own. Once it attracts followers, it heads off in a specific direction, hopefully the one you intended! While there are ways to get an Instagram account back on track, if mistakes have been made - we will talk about that in a later chapter - it is always preferential if your account has been built from the ground up with the correct approach.

Preparation is *everything*.

Before signing up for your Instagram account, it is best to have definitive answers to these questions:

- What is my main goal for my Instagram account?

- Which demographic is my Instagram account directed towards?

- Is my Instagram account part of a bigger picture?

- What is my branding?

By answering these questions, you will have a much better chance to establish a successful Instagram account as quickly as possible.

What is my main goal for my Instagram account?

Think of your Instagram as the focal point of a business. What is a business most concerned with? We may not like to think of it in such cold terms, but business success is intimately connected to brand growth and sales. If a business does not focus on these things, then it will slowly diminish until it is no longer viable. However, we need not think about Instagram purely in terms of sales, though monetization as you will see later in this book is an important factor. *You* may have a different goal in mind.

Common Instagram goals include:

1. **Message**: With this goal, your Instagram will be focused on conveying a central idea. This could be a political message. It could also be a personal message, such as an uplifting mantra. Alternatively, it may be a message about a product or service. The concept of message is very important

within Instagram and all social media marketing. If you know the type of message that you want to convey, this will give you a fantastic foundation on which to build your entire Instagram account and campaigns.

2. **Meaning**: You yourself may be searching for meaning in your life. Maybe you are wanting to use your Instagram account to explore aspects of your life and may find that the entire endeavor of having a social media account is purely there for you to discover this meaning yourself. This can be helped with interactions with other users and ideas from other Instagram accounts that you may see. Meaning is not just important in terms of Instagram, it is also a fundamental aspect of life, which must be tended to. For some, Instagram opens up the possibility of exploring this meaning.

3. **Support**: Another Instagram goal could be to use your account as some form of support. Now, what I mean by this is that your Instagram is there to support some other endeavor. Let us say that you have a product that you really believe in and you want to increase its exposure and sales. Instagram is a fantastic way to do this. Perhaps you have a blog, or a book, or a Youtube channel; perhaps even another social media page, which you want to support, Instagram can allow you to do all

these things by funneling people to your desired destination.

4. **Fame**: Last but certainly by no means least, Instagram is undoubtedly a means to achieve a level of fame. Whether that is through travelling or being part of the beauty industry, Instagram is used to generate attention and lasting celebrity. There is no shame in using Instagram in this way, and in fact, if you are looking to establish yourself as a known face or public figure, then Instagram is perhaps the best of all social media through which to achieve this goal.

I want you to think about what your main goal is. Most importantly, I want you to write it down on a piece of paper and keep it nearby whenever you are working on your Instagram account. Open up that piece of paper, look at that goal and understand that your goal must feed into every single post you make. This is the foundation on which everything else you do and on which Instagram relies.

Which demographic is my Instagram account directed towards?

Another key consideration is which demographic you are aiming at. A demographic is simply a slice of an audience. Imagine, if you will, that you restore classic cars. You are using your Instagram account to add much needed exposure to your business. The images you post, as well as your stories, show the beautiful and precise nature of the restoration work you carry out. However, this type of Instagram campaign is not going to be of interest to everyone. It is going to be of interest specifically to only a portion of Instagram users.

But which Instagram users?

Finding out exactly which demographic you should be focusing on will be discussed at a later stage in this book, but for now I want you to have a general idea of who your content is being aimed at. In the above example, it would be people who are interested in old cars and restoration work. More than that, you may also think that the majority of that group will be within a specific age bracket. Just for this example, say that your experience in your business tells you that most of the people who are interested in restoring classic cars are aged 50 and up. This then gives you a great idea of how to target Instagram posts. You know then that you are trying to hit two ideas:

1. Those who are interested in old cars and restoration.

2. People who are aged 50 and up.

These two points then will help you decide how to present your Instagram posts. You will find something called *indirect marketing* (which we will discuss throughout this book) extremely useful and this is a great place to use such an idea. For our car example, you might focus on nostalgic elements of people's lives who are older than 50. Perhaps even some aspects that are not connected to cars, but will move and entice people of that age group to be interested in your Instagram account. You are not directly marketing the cars, but you are bringing in people within the demographic which you feel will be most successful for you.

There are ways to figure out which demographic you should be targeting and again we will discuss this later, but for now it is a good technique to have a general idea for whom your content is intended. You will then be able to cater your content on Instagram for those specific people. Just like figuring out what your main goal is for your Instagram account, the demographic that you are targeting will also inform many of the decisions you make about your Instagram campaigns in the future.

Is my Instagram account part of a bigger picture?

When introducing you to the ideas behind your Instagram account at the start of this chapter, we talked about goals. One of the example goals we gave for an Instagram creator, was the idea that your Instagram account can be used to support a larger framework. That it has a secondary importance. It is not an account just for itself, but rather for your business or your website or some other thing which lives outside of your Instagram account.

Related to this, I want you to think about whether your account is part of a bigger picture not. If it is to promote materials and other content outside of

Instagram, then this will feed into the types of posts you make. You will use something called a call to action (CTA). A call to action is marketing speak for the moment where you want your viewer/customer to make a decision and carry out an action. This can be clicking a link to something outside of your Instagram account.

Perhaps your marketing a discount that you are offering elsewhere. Or maybe you are being paid to post promotional material for a third party and you are providing links for your Instagram followers to click in order to access their products/services. Whichever it is, think about how your Instagram account can be used to filter people through a CTA to content outside of your Instagram profile. This is a huge consideration, especially for those who are monetising their posts, and it is important to highlight this because, again, if you are using your Instagram profile to connect it to materials, content, or products outside of your profile, then this will change the type of posts you are making.

What is my branding?

The final consideration to setting up an effective Instagram account, is understanding branding. Branding refers to the way you present your content so that users:

1. Recognize instantly that the content is yours.

2. Understand implicitly the type of message or product you are selling.

Branding is more than just a watermark, a logo, or a slogan. It incorporates all of these things but also so much more. Your branding is even more important because Instagram is largely a visual medium. That means the colours, the style and the content of your images directly convey messages and meanings to your audience. It is critical that you think about the type of branding that you will have on your Instagram account.

Now, you may already have a solid idea of your branding as you are using your Instagram account to support or link to other endeavors, which already have their own branding. However, you could also be starting from the beginning without a fully formed idea of how to forge the most enticing branding for what you are trying to achieve. Branding is something which, and it cannot be stressed enough, needs to be consistently conveyed. You may find that something does not work quite so well in the beginning, but the worst thing you can do is to constantly chop and change the type of branding you are using on your posts. You want to make sure that you give your branding enough time to breathe and establish itself. Unless you have the best marketing on the planet, it is rare for branding to make a huge impact straightaway. It is an accumulative process, as your followers click on each post; seeing a consistent use of style and imagery to the point that eventually it will instantly connect you to any piece of content which uses that exact same branding.

Branding is intimately connected to the message of your product and the meaning which you want to convey in your posts, so it is an essential part of what you are doing. It also lays the foundation for growth well into the future. If people come to trust your branding or see it as representative of quality, then they are far more likely to be involved in other endeavors or other Instagram campaigns which you carry out, because the branding suggests to them that what you are doing is worthwhile and reliable.

Your branding, then, will affect how you present your material on Instagram. But do not worry, it is difficult to get this right straight off the bat. Instagram pros suggest doing some test campaigns where you post six or seven pieces of content to see what people respond to. Eventually, you may have to tweak or change the branding if it does not work over a longer period, but it is counter productive to do so immediately just because something does not attract success instantaneously.

We will talk more about branding when we are exploring the monetization of Instagram posts later in this book, but it is helpful if you continue to think about the type of branding you are going to use throughout your Instagram career.

Conclusion

We have broadly covered the essential, foundational ideas behind a great, successful Instagram profile. But now we want to deal with the specifics of leveraging these ideas to create Instagram posts which have impact. You should continually reappraise the concepts in this chapter as you are creating your Instagram content and using more advanced techniques. No matter what, you will always be able to whittle down what you are doing to the key components of the message, meaning, support, or fame. Sometimes it will be a combination of these ideas, but you will always be able to use these as an anchor for your Instagram content.

Now we can push on to both basic posting strategies and growing your audience.

CHAPTER 2: BASIC POSTING STRATEGIES

In this chapter, we are going to open the book up and explore basic posting strategies. We will not waste precious time going through a step-by-step process of setting up your Instagram account, this is fairly intuitive and there are many books which deal with such things, but what we are going to do is to establish good, healthy practices on Instagram. Even if you are an experienced veteran on Instagram, you may have picked up bad habits. This chapter then is for those who are just starting out and those who have been using Instagram for a while, but who are open to new ways of doing things.

The good practices in Instagram marketing which you will learn in this chapter, will help you develop social media posts that are both captivating and effective at funneling viewers towards your end goal, as explored in the previous chapter.

Let us get to it!

First Impressions Count

Growing up, you might have been told that it is what is underneath which matters, but in the world of social media first impressions count. That is not to say that your deep meaning or complex message is not important - they are - but these aspects of your Instagram account can only be successful if the first impression you make with an audience member is a positive one. Imagine a situation where all of your Instagram posts are successful, but your latest one conveys a negative image of you or your product. Well, there will be people who will encounter you on Instagram for the first time through that post. Their impression of you will not be a positive one, and therefore you will hurt your brand and lose out on a potential long-time follower. This is also true of your profile overall.

Ask yourself, what is the first thing a new follower will see when clicking on your profile page. They may see a short biography, perhaps a profile picture that you have selected to represent your best side, and a list of your most recent posts. However, in that short introduction of images, recent posts, and bio, you want your followers to have a positive impression of who you are and what they can expect from your Instagram account. This is true of your Instagram posts, which should give potential followers a taste of what to expect from you.

Therefore, you want the first impression to be one which grabs the attention of new and old followers, conveying something about you or a product, and grows your brand recognition by exposing people to your branding.

Slow and Steady Wins the Race

You should be aware of social media burnout as you chart out your posting strategy. Underestimating is one of the biggest and most common mistakes people make online. The relentless posting of content, the stress of feeling that you always have an audience to satisfy. These combine to create a powerfully negative effect on content creators. This is something that you should be aware of. When it comes to posting, regular content is a must, but you need not burn yourself out through the process.

If you post very seldom, however, you cannot expect to grow your audience significantly. If you *do* post far too much, then many of your posts will be overlooked. They will become background noise and your followers may even be annoyed by having to keep up. Slow and steady wins the race. There is a middle ground which you should shoot for which will both grow your Instagram account and protect you from having any sort of personal burnout. Posting once a day works well for many people on Instagram. It allows 24 hours for a post to be seen and even go viral, and it does not necessarily have to take up too much of your time if you have other concerns.

The top brands post on average about 1.5 times each day, so that is about 11 posts per week. If you can keep that schedule going, then you will find it to be beneficial for you. The minimum posting schedule which is effective, is roughly about once every 3 days. The caveat to that is that, if the type of content you post takes much longer to produce, then you have to accept the reality that you will not be able to post regularly, unless it is small updates in between larger projects.

Make it Fun

You might think this goes without saying, but you would be surprised how many Instagram influencers avoid this piece of advice, and at their peril. Your posts should be engaging. Of course, you can cover serious topics, and your brand may be specifically dealing with an area which is difficult to present in a fun way. However, at all times you should try to be entertaining. Boring content will get you nowhere, and in fact it will hurt your brand.

Furthermore, it can be annoying if every second post is a promotional item. Followers want to feel a connection to you through Instagram, and if they feel that they are constantly being bombarded with advertising, then they will feel like they are being used. Make your content fun and engaging by mixing up the type of material that you are posting. Be funny, quirky, and show personality through your posts. This will allow your followers to make a personal connection with you which will then convert them into fans, and even paying customers.

Above all else make your content entertaining, and always remember who your content is intended for. If it is not intended for people with an interest in a specific topic, especially if the topic is controversial, then it may be best to avoid it. Conversely, your audience may thrive on controversy and difficult topics, but you must present these in an entertaining, captivating way.

Live Means Authentic

When Facebook, YouTube and the first generation of social media platforms were developed, content was viewed as pre-recorded as opposed to live. With the advent of Twitch and other live streaming platforms, Instagram, Facebook and other social media sites are now heavily promoting their live streaming capabilities. This is something that as an Instagram user you should embrace in order to be contemporary. Most successful Instagram users make strategic and fun use of the ability to livestream.

Instagram has a fantastic live broadcast feature which has grown to become a full competitor in many ways to YouTube. But it is more than just about being innovative when using live streaming in your Instagram posts. Broadcasting live creates a spontaneous, natural, and authentic experience for your Instagram followers. With so many Instagram images being doctored and enhanced with Photoshop, live broadcasts allow followers to see the real you in hopefully entertaining fashion.

When authenticity means more now than ever in social media circles, it is important to incorporate live broadcasts into your Instagram campaigns. This can take the form of a simple out and about vlog, to question and answer segments which are a great way to engage with your audience. Live streaming is also an effective way to see who your super fans are, the ones who will take the time to watch and engage with you as you go live. This will further help you identify who your key demographic is.

The Power of Disappearing Content

A key component of any interaction between a creator and consumer is one of scarcity. Economic books are filled full of insightful lessons about how scarcity increases demand. Just think of gold and how precious it is to every culture in the world. It is because of its scarcity that it has become precious. This is true of Instagram's story feature. In response to services like Snapchat, Instagram has released a component of its service where you can post to your story timeline. These pieces of content can be images or videos. But the defining feature is that they only last 24 hours after being uploaded. This creates an impetus for your followers to watch and engage with your story before it disappears.

By creating a limited window for one of your stories to be enjoyed, you make your followers feel special, chosen in some way, because they are enjoying content that will no longer be there shortly after. They are privileged, gaining access to something which is a slice of life. One of the great things about the stories feature is that it allows you to post multiple times throughout the day without it flooding your users or blocking your other content posts. However, this does not mean you should post 30 times a day. Instead, posting a handful of times on your story timeline is more than enough on any given day.

Regularly posting to your story creates an intimate connection with your audience, and encourages them to stay up-to-date with your Instagram account, otherwise they would miss out - and no one wants to do that.

Capture Those Captions

The images and videos you post are of course important, but what is often overlooked is the use of captions which accompany them to convey new information. More than that, captions can contain little moments or inspirational thoughts which add value to your visual content, perhaps even explaining the context of said content.

Most importantly, you can include hashtags in your captions for each post you make. Hashtags are incredibly important when it comes to increasing overall engagement with your content. This also allows people who are not aware of your Instagram to find your account through the hashtags that they are following. This could be a wide-ranging topic or a hashtag which is connected to a temporary trend. If you use hashtags which are already in existence, then you have access to a large following, this can be a way to find new audience members. But you can also create your own hashtag and be a leader. Then that hashtag becomes synonymous with your own brand. A combination of both approaches is most useful.

Use Your Users

Your followers can be thought of as consumers or users of the service you are providing. They enjoy what you produce and in return you get to reach one of the main goals that we talked about in chapter 1. However, your followers or users are way more important than just that. You should think of them as the lifeblood of what you are trying to achieve on Instagram. Without a consistent influx of followers who stay with you over time, your Instagram account will stagnate and not reach its full potential.

Continual interaction with your followers, therefore, is a great way to ensure that they continue to follow you. This could be through a number of methods including giveaways and competitions, featuring long-time followers on live streams, question-and-answer posts, and simple responses to comments via text.

One of the most useful ways of leveraging your audience is to employ something called UGC. UGC simply means *user generated content*. By running promotional posts asking for user submissions, you can then use this user generated content to further propel your Instagram account in terms of popularity. A promotion such as this could be asking users to use a hashtag you have developed and make a post under a specific topic linking to your account. You could also then pick the best UGC posts and feature them on your Instagram page, helping them gain exposure to followers themselves. These posts could also be challenge related such as encouraging people to eat a certain kind of food and to take a picture of it, or to reach a specific fitness milestone while running a marathon.

You just have to use your imagination to create a promotional post which is going to bring in user interaction and user submitted posts.

Rinse and Repeat

Whatever your goal is on Instagram, say it is to sell a product, you are not going to maximise your results based on just one post. You will have to make posts about the same product, service, or topic more than once in order to gain the type of traction that you need. This is a rinse and repeat process. However, as we mentioned earlier, you should not flood your followers with constant promotional posts. That means that you have to box clever when it comes to choosing the frequency with which you post about a specific product topic.

There is no hard or fast rule to this; however, posting about such a product or service once per five posts, when you post regularly, is a good place to start. Measure the response you get and if you see followers being annoyed by the promotional posts, loosen it off a little bit and space out the posts to a degree.

Conclusion

In this chapter, we have covered the foundations of basic posting strategies. There are other best practices, but if you look at experienced and successful Instagram posters, you will find that they have based their campaigns on these aspects either deliberately or just through luck. By incorporating and thinking about these aspects each time you post, you will significantly increase the success rate of your Instagram posts and profile in general.

Chapter 3: Growing Your Audience

Now that we have established setting goals for your Instagram profile and a basic foundational strategy for making posts, it is time to look specifically at growing an audience. Growing an audience on Instagram involves meeting three requirements:

1. Enticing people to your posts and profile.

2. Earning followers through this content.

3. Encouraging those followers to become long-term fans and/or paying customers.

In this chapter, we are going to explore these three questions so that you have a good understanding of how to reach the people who are going to propel your Instagram profile towards longevity and success.

Meet Expectations

As with all social media platforms, Instagram has its own posting etiquette. This etiquette arises out of common trends and the way people interact and use the platform. Over time, users become accustomed to the way that Instagram is used and, therefore, they implicitly build expectations about how an Instagram post should look, be formatted and be experienced. We will get to being a *renegade* next and exploring innovative approaches to posting, but especially when you are starting out, posting in a way that users will understand and expect is a good habit to get into.

This includes the way that Instagram is used as a primarily visual medium. It could also be the language that you use, and the hashtags which you employ, along with the layout of your posts. All of these are going to feed into this idea of expectation, providing signposts which you can follow towards producing content which meets the needs of your potential followers. The best thing you can do to learn what these guidelines are, is to find fellow Instagram users who are established within your chosen niche, look at how they are making posts and laying them out, and then emulate this to a degree.

One of the ways you can do this is through the use of filters on your photographs. Images are usually presented in a certain way on Instagram. In a recent study by Iconosquare, which is a service which provides metrics to Instagram users, it was found that there are 10 approaches to the look of an Instagram image which users come to expect.

These are:

1. **No filter**

2. **Clarendon**

3. **Juno**

4. **Lark**

5. **Ludwig**

6. **Gingham**

7. **Valencia**

8. **X-Pro II**

9. **Lo-fi**

10. **Amaro**

By incorporating popular filters into your posts, users will implicitly "get" your content. This is just one example of how you can meet the expectations of Instagram followers.

Break Expectations

Once you have a great feel for the style and layout of posts within your niche and across Instagram generally, you then need to distinguish yourself from the pack. It is important to become a successful Instagram influencer through *differentiation*. To be a leader, not a sheep. By learning the standards and norms of Instagram posts, you should then have a good idea of what you can do differently. In some cases, this will be merely adapting the existing styles slightly, changing them in a subtle way to suit you and your branding.

If you feel like being bolder, then you may wish to completely break from established traditions. It is recommended to do this only once you have been on Instagram for awhile and have really familiarized yourself with the usual way of doing things. Once you master that, then you can include your own expression. This will involve **font choice**, **image content**, **filter use**, the creation of **brand-new hashtags**, and the **innovative planning** of topics to engage with your audience and bring in new followers.

Collaboration

In the early days of YouTube, users soon realised that collaborating with each other was a great way to:

1. Create new content distinct in some way from your usual output.

2. Gain access to another YouTuber's audience.

3. Push yourself creatively and learn new ways of doing things.

4. To lower the burden of content making, sharing it with another person and therefore producing content without having to invest more time.

5. Increase your search rankings.

All of this is true for Instagram. Collaborating is a fantastic way for you to push yourself and learn how to create new forms of content, while in many cases lowering the amount of work you have to do because the workload is shared. The best thing about collaborating is that it is an effective way to network and make friends within your niche. Then when your content is produced on Instagram, those you have networked with in this way will be more inclined to simply share your content organically without being asked.

Cross Promotion

Speaking of gaining access to another Instagram influencer's audience, general cross promotion is always to be encouraged when attempting to grow your Instagram following. The simplest form of cross promotion is simply agreeing to share each other's content.

Cross promotion includes:

1. Agreeing with another influencer to publicly speak about their profile and/or products in a positive way.

2. Exchanging a defined number of promoted posts for each other - if you are paid to do this, you are legally required to include that it is a paid post in the description.

3. Posting links to each other's Instagram profiles on other social media accounts and websites.

4. Leaving comments on each other's profiles and posts.

There are loads of other ways to cross promote. Many of them venture more into the realm of **collaboration**, so combine cross promotion with collaboration whenever possible.

It is advisable to approach a number of Instagram users with a similar following to yourself rather than approaching someone with millions of followers. The reason for this is that it is unlikely the most popular Instagram influencers will want to cross promote with you unless they absolutely love what you are doing. They want to get something out of the cross promotion, and if that does not include either products, money, or being exposed to another significant audience, then they will not feel that it is worth their time. In the beginning, it is best to start small. Once you do some cross promotions with similarly sized Instagram accounts, then you can gauge what is working for you what is not. As your audience grows, you will then be able to offer greater cross promotion ideas to more popular Instagram users.

Use Your Best Times

There is great debate amongst Instagram users with regards to what is the best time to post content. If there was a magical time where most users would be exposed to your content, then everybody would post at that time. That would then probably undermine the whole endeavor because once more your post would get lost in the noise. The truth is, **there is no one size fits all approach to posting at the most popular time**. However, this does not mean that you should not pay attention to when your posts are being most successful.

There is a difference between a general best time for *everyone* on Instagram and the best time for *you* individually. Your individual best time will absolutely exist. In fact, you will probably find that there are a couple of timeframes or windows of opportunity which will work best for you. In order to discover what your best, most fruitful times are when posting content, you need to make several posts and experiment with different time slots systematically. You can measure this through Instagram's own available analytics, which we will explore in a moment, but also through several services online such as Iconosquare, which offers an in depth analysis of your posting habits. You will be able to see which times are most beneficial for you. Target those times and reap the rewards.

See What Works

In the same way that you can monitor which time is most fruitful for you, you can also look to see which types of content are most successful for you. A great way to measure this is both in terms of views and engagement. If people are responding to your content, then you are definitely going in the right direction. At first, you will be able to just eyeball which types of content are working best for you. Over time, however, as you build a long list of posts, it becomes slightly more difficult to analyse what is working best for you.

An effective route to gain detailed access to your statistics and analytics which will show various information about who is interacting with your content, how they are interacting with it, and how often, is to register an Instagram business account. The analytics provided through an Instagram business account will give you valuable insights which are unavailable elsewhere. You will quickly be able to see the type of content which is most popular amongst your followers and what is bringing in new fans.

Once you find out the types of content which are working best for you, rinse and repeat. Keep at it, post similar yet engaging content, and you will build a larger audience.

Ride the Trend

Lastly, you should pay particular attention to trends. Observe the competition, see what people who are interested in your niche are doing and saying and gravitating towards, and then build your Instagram campaigns around this information. There is a concept in marketing known as "alignment". Essentially, all this means is that you see a trend and you align yourself with it. This could be a topic, cause, a product that people are having fun with, or even a way of presenting images and videos to the public.

Trends also can be time specific or connected to definable events. Halloween, Christmas, Thanksgiving and other periods are often hotbeds of activity on Instagram. It is a good idea to develop a plan for these times throughout the year, so that you are not left behind by other people competing in your niche. And it does not need to be a huge celebration, either. It could be International Pirate Day or International Meme Day; whatever it is, try and have fun with it and you will attract followers who are interested in those celebrations and jokes. Alternatively, focus on important causes such as Aids Awareness Day or other such causes which you feel passionate about, and post something related to this on that chosen day.

Conclusion

In this chapter, we have covered a good amount of ideas on how to grow your audience. There are many more techniques out there, so it is a good idea to continue your study in this area. You will also find that certain strategies will work for you better than others. This tends to be specific to your niche and your post content. So, do not be downhearted if one approach does not yield a large number of new followers. You will get there in the end. You just have to believe and try new things. Constantly adapt and never give up.

If you're enjoying this book, I would appreciate it if you went to the place of purchase and left a short positive review. Thank you

Part 2: Beyond the Basics

Chapter 4: The Power of Stories

Storytelling is an ancient art form. It goes back to the beginning of our very species. It is no surprise then that in the 21st-century, storytelling has found new and fertile ground within the medium of social media. Indeed, as we have mentioned, Instagram has its very own method of conveying storytelling to an audience entitled, simply: "Stories".

In this chapter, we are going to discuss the power of stories and how they can be used through Instagram's stories feature to build an audience and extend the overall reach of your Instagram account.

Stories Bring Engagement

Hundreds of millions of people use stories on Instagram each and every day. It was inspired by a Snapchat feature, and allows users to post content such as images and videos which will only last for 24 hours. It is important that you realise that everyone uses them. Businesses, celebrities, and your humble day-to-day Instagram user. As Instagram is owned by Facebook, a similar feature has rolled out on that as well, which allows you to cross post your content which is extremely handy if you have different audiences on each social media account.

Just how powerful are stories? On Instagram, one in five stories on average receive a direct response. That is a powerful statistic of engagement. You cannot afford to overlook the stories feature or you will be left behind by those competing in your space. Some do, because it involves more regular updates and they feel this is not worth their time, but when used strategically, the benefits are impressive. And you need not experience burnout, as stories tend to be short and easy to produce with a lack of polish.

Valuable Stories

While stories are incredibly powerful, this does not mean by simply posting *anything* you will be successful. Like any form of communication on social media, the most successful posts are ones which are thought out and targeted. More than this, stories which work well are the ones which provide *value* to the viewer. If your stories are boring or about nothing in particular, and show no personality, then followers are less likely to continue watching your story feed. It is important then that you keep this idea of <u>value</u> at the centre of every story campaign or post you make. A simple rule of thumb is that if it does not provide value of any kind, do not post it.

But how do you know your post has value? Here are a few elements of value which are worth exploring while you experiment with different posts on your story timeline. Look to expand upon these and you will create value for your followers:

1. **Be a storyteller**: Being a storyteller on Instagram does not mean starting every post with "once upon a time", but it does mean telling a clear and simple story to your audience. Your story, is a collection of ideas and images. A simple story, concisely told, is easier to remember. For this reason, keep your stories pure. Do not clutter them with too many ideas. This is especially true if you have a CTA to which you want your audience to respond. And always prioritise the experience of the viewer. You want your story to have a beginning, middle, and an end, which holds meaning and provides some use to   those watching.

2. **Do not be fake**: In the world of Instagram, the manipulation of appearance and character is everywhere. Instagram users continue to present the best possible version of themselves, but they do so in such a way at times which renders the experience sterile. At worst, the person appears inauthentic and fake. To stand out from the crowd these days and to truly engage with people, it is important that you are sincere and   believable. It is also important that you are relatable. Your stories then should contain this authenticity. They need not be overly polished or produced. They are a slice of

life, a moment in time which you are sharing from your life, carrying with it a message, pure and simple. Do not strive for perfection, strive to be relatable and easily understood.

3. **Have a point**: As stated above, just because you have a story timeline this does not mean that you should continually bombard it with useless, pointless posts. While it can be charming to simply post a moment from your day, and this will absolutely help your authenticity in doing so; trying to have a central idea behind what your story represents most of the time. Is your post a clip of you buying something in town? Then, be sure to show what you are buying. Just walking down a street quietly looking at the camera is not going to engage your audience. Neither is waffling, unless you are an experienced and talented raconteur. Before you switch your camera on, and certainly before you post, make sure you have a central point to what you are about to capture. Always plan ahead and have a clear CTA at the end of your story if that is its purpose. Remember as well that while we talk about planning ahead, this does not mean that there is no room for spontaneity. Try to add a natural, *real* element to everything you do. Just do so with a point in mind.

4. **Be creative**: As we have established, researching the standard ways of doing things helps you both meet the expectations of Instagram users and understand where you could differentiate yourself from the crowd. When planning out your stories, try to use them in a way that is innovative and different. If that means you are capturing a different type of content from anyone else, fantastic. More than anything, it will probably mean that you are showing your own individuality and individual personality. Think of ways to showcase this, think of your strengths, think of the things that your friends and loved ones love about you and try to show it to the world. This is your individuality. If you have a product you are selling, then likewise, show what you love about that product and why people should get excited about it, why they need it in their lives, but always do so in a creative way. Boredom is the enemy.

Story Ideas

As this book is intended for more intermediate Instagram users, we will assume that you know how to post stories, but if you are unaware how to do this, there are many tutorials available online. You can also find Instagram's own guide on this subject, here. It is a fairly intuitive process. What is not intuitive, however, is how to use the stories feature to reliably grow your audience and improve the reach of your Instagram account.

Thankfully the research is in, and we can highlight several approaches you can use to truly leverage the power of storytelling. These include:

- **Life posts**: These types of story ideas are especially important to individual Instagram users who are their brand. If you are promoting yourself as the brand in which your audience should invest their time and money, then life posts are essential. These can be little video diaries with your thoughts about an issue. Most of the time, they will be posts about the day-to-day things you are doing in your life or the issues you face, however, not presented in a boring way, but rather a charming, informative way. These especially work well when you have not had the time to craft larger more complex stories. Create that personal connection between you and your audience by showing who you are and what your daily experiences are like. Just make sure that this is presented in an interesting, connective way. These types of posts can be videos or images. If you are running a business, this does not mean you cannot make life posts to your company story. In fact you can, and effectively. An example would be focusing on specific individuals within your company and experiences they wish to convey.

- **Tutorials**: Tutorial posts are a great way to increase your audience and provide extensive value through lessons which people can then incorporate in their lives. These tutorials often should be connected to the type of brand you are developing. If you are involved in the beauty industry, for example, then you could make a tutorial about eyeshadow. Likewise, if you are a painter, perhaps you could show a short tutorial about a certain technique that you use. If you are a company which sells computer technology, then a tutorial would work well which shows how to use either your product or another related one. Tutorials add great value and are usually well received by followers, as they are receiving useful information for free.

- **Adventure posts**: These types of posts are similar to life posts in certain ways. They involve more elaborate posts about an activity which you are taking part in, usually a special one-off moment. Alternatively, it could be a location you are going to. Perhaps you are visiting a famous landmark. You could also be abseiling down a cliffside and showing your GoPro footage. But an adventure post does not have to always be so grand. It can also be a story about a trip to the cinema or finding something funny while you are out and about running errands. These adventure posts make viewers feel as though they have a deep connection with you; that they are going on the experience with you. If you are a business rather than presenting individuals as your brand, then likewise you can show people using your product in interesting ways and in interesting locations, or show a staff member who uses your Instagram account going on an adventure of their own to add a personal face to your company.

- **Behind the scenes**: Numerous Instagram users post stories about behind-the-scenes. These are tidbits, images, and videos about the making of your content. If you are a model at a photo shoot, then perhaps you will upload a video showing you at the set. If you are a filmmaker, then perhaps you are showing a behind-the-scenes moment with your actors. Again, behind-the-scenes does not have to be grand. It could be showing your setup in your bedroom that you use to record the vlogs. Behind-the-scenes footage again connects the audience, showing that you are a human being, that you are willing to show your real side, and this brings in authenticity through being less polished than the final product.

- **Deliver news**: Another type of story you could tell involves either commenting or announcing news. Perhaps there is an election on which you will be voting in, or maybe a tragic event which you want to give your opinion on. More removed from the seriousness of real life, maybe your favourite TV show has been cancelled or renewed for a new season and you want to tell people about it. Delivering news to your followers encourages them to comment with their own opinions. Just be wary that in this day and age, the divide between people, especially in terms of politics is huge. So, try to promote a more positive take on things unless a specific political perspective is important to you and your brand.

- **Brand announcements**: If you have any announcement about you, your Instagram account, other social media profiles, or your brand in general, your stories are a great medium through which to keep your followers "in the know". A great technique in achieving this is to pre-empt an official announcement. For example, let us say you are about to launch a new T-shirt, you might show yourself wearing a T-shirt on your story just before making the full, polished Instagram post about it. This again makes your audience feel as though they are closer to you than the ordinary fan, getting the scoop before everyone else. Also, if there are any issues with your brand such as growing complaints about a product/service or issue, then you can quickly address this via a story to minimise the damage before making an official statement.

- **Make lists**: List making is very successful at garnering engagement. You could list your favourite 10 action movies or perhaps your top ten first date dislikes. Whatever it is, you are sure to get people commenting on the entries you have included. They may even post their own top 10 list in response. This works really well at provoking discussion about a topic. Just make sure the topic is interesting, and not about your top 10 favourite socks. Although, that could be funny.

- **Invite a takeover**: Takeovers are a great way to include other creators in your story. You can allow other people to post to your story after vetting the content. You could even announce that your story timeline is going to be taken over by another Instagram user for 24 hours. Alternatively, you could run a competition allowing fans to start posting content to your story. Obviously, providing direct access to your account is not a great idea, so you would have to vet each piece of content before it was uploaded. However, takeovers are fun even for larger companies. You could run a competition asking people to post content about using one of your products in a certain way. Then the winners get to post to your story timeline.

- **Shoutouts**: Lastly, giving regular shoutouts to your most engaging fans, helps forge the impression that you really care about the people who are watching your content. Fans will enjoy seeing that you value them, and this will present a good impression of you to the larger world who may not be aware of you, your product or brand just yet. This helps promote a feeling of community around your Instagram account.

Conclusion

We have covered quite a bit of ground in chapter 4. You have learned the power of stories, how to add value to your stories on Instagram, along with several examples of the types of stories you can post. Using this information, you will be able to build a larger audience and bring in new followers, as well as you show value to your existing fans. Your story timeline is a powerful means to communicate with the world, use it, but do so wisely and with value at its core.

Chapter 5: Advanced Posting Strategies

In this chapter we are going to explore more advanced posting strategies. So far we have established the importance of good housekeeping, basic posting strategies, and leveraging the stories feature on Instagram to fully maximise your return on your content. While all of these combined provide a fantastic foundation for any Instagram account, there is always room to grow. These advanced posting strategies will point you in the direction to expand your approach with new ideas and techniques.

It must always be remembered that your journey as an Instagram creator is a perpetual one, where you must continue the learning process in the continual search of growth and success. Let us now explore a handful of critical advanced posting strategies, which you can use as a basis to continue your Instagram journey.

Connected Campaigns

Connected campaigns are one of the most powerful advanced posting strategies on Instagram. So far, we have focused on your relationships with your followers, taking into consideration the goals which you hope to achieve. These have largely been based on single posts, however, a connected campaign is much broader than that. A connected campaign includes two major components:

1. **Internal content.**

2. **External content.**

Internal content refers to anything which is posted within Instagram. **External content** deals with anything which ties into your Instagram campaign but which is outwith it. An example of an internal piece of content would be an image you post on Instagram, while an example of external content would be a video posted on Facebook about the content of your Instagram image.

Connected campaigns can run for just a few posts or across a longer period with numerous pieces of content. Imagine that you are a games design company using Instagram to promote your latest game. You would probably run a connected campaign with materials such as posters, sneak peaks, and tidbits of information regarding the game you are about to release. These would be posted to your Instagram account and your other social media profiles. You would then move through the release of the game, posting reviews and let's plays from prominent Youtubers. Perhaps those youtubers have Instagram accounts themselves, and you work out a deal with them so that they are posting material about your game, and linking to your Instagram account. This is a great example of using internal content and external content to promote a product. More than that, it shows the beauty of the connected campaign.

What is most important for a connected campaign, is that it contains a **content theme**. When planning a connected campaign, the theme of the content should remain paramount over all else. An example of this would be a series of Instagram posts about recycling plastic. Imagine that this is an issue you feel passionately about, and so you want to post a campaign of posts about this issue. When planning out those posts then, you would be constantly thinking about the theme of those posts.

To strengthen the connective tissue between these posts, you can:

- Link to previous posts with each subsequent release. This allows your users to follow the chain of thought that you're presenting.

- Use a hashtag to curate all that content together.

- Use the same slogan, visual style, or image theme throughout your campaign.

Connected campaigns show that you are developing as an Instagram poster, with a greater understanding of producing content which has value, and is long-lasting. These connected posts could last any amount of time, but it is a very good idea to break the campaign up into quarters and re-evaluate the success of the campaign each quarter. You can then alter your approach or even abandon the campaign before investing more in it if the campaign has not produced the results you are looking for.

Content Calendar

One of the key components of a developing Instagram user, is to take organisational skills seriously. Your posts can no longer be added on a whim. Perhaps you do plan out your posts as we have talked about in previous chapters, but creating something known as a **content calendar** allows you to plan a strategy which extends well into the future.

A content calendar is a blueprint for your entire Instagram approach. It can also include content from any number of other sources including your other social media accounts and websites. Think of it as a map which charts the way for you towards a more successful Instagram account. It is recommended that a content calendar should take into account the next 12 months. This will allow you to plan well in advance for special events such as Christmas or taking a holiday.

Using a content calendar is not just about writing down the posts that you are going to make, it is about seeing the bigger picture about where your content is going. By charting out all of the future posts you are going to make within a defined period, you can see whether you are being deficient in some areas. Perhaps your content is video light, and so you realize you need to focus more on that. Alternatively, your content calendar may show that you are not being as consistent with your releases as you thought. You may also realize that you are investing time in a type of content which is not producing results for you.

Creating a content calendar is fairly simple. You can do it using the calendar function or an app on your computer or mobile device. However, using a service such as Trello is a great way to plan out your calendar function. This provides a number of organizational tools for you, but at its most basic level you will be able to assign post ideas to specific dates. You will also be able to write up lists of potential ideals. This is a great option for working in the cloud if you have a team with you. Each person can then add their thoughts or ideas about your content to the Trello calendar.

Use your content calendar to forge a path ahead and develop a plan of action. Too many Instagram users fall foul of not planning ahead enough. Organization is key, especially as your account grows and you are then dealing with many followers.

Supplementary Apps

Finally, it is important to go one step beyond when crafting your content on Instagram. We talked about the most used filters earlier and how you should familiarize yourself with these to meet the expectations of Instagram users. However, you must also show that you are putting more effort into your Instagram account than many others. You can add more value by staying abridged of other applications and techniques which can differentiate your content.

There are many services and apps which will allow you to create a more unique brand with content specifically designed for your followers. A few of these apps are provided by Instagram themselves. Instagram has developed a few applications which will help you in this area. Three of these are:

1. **Boomerang**: An app designed to make fun moments and capture the unexpected. Much like a GIF, the Boomerang app creates a mini video which can loop back and forward. These videos capture a specific moment and add a level of quirk to your video content. The app also allows you to create compelling video content without investing a lot of time. It essentially captures a burst of 10 photographs from your phone camera and then converts this into a small video. Try to use this in a creative way to add value to your posts.

2. **Layout**: Another app, which Instagram has developed, is the Layout app. This is a great way to remix your content and post an overarching idea in one post. It allows you to combine a bunch of different images in a collage of sorts. You can edit the layout to add your own unique spin to it. This is a great option if you are wanting to showcase a bunch of photographs from the one event or about the one group of people. Again, it

adds value because it goes beyond just a simple image.

3. <u>Hyperlapse</u>: This app allows you to create amazing time-lapse videos. You could show the clouds above rolling past at a fast rate or the stars at night moving together in harmony. You could show the number of people gathering together on a beach for a party moving around and interacting with each other at speed. Or how about the buzzing traffic lights of cars throughout the city streaking across the scene to unknown places. The opportunities are limitless with an app like Hyperlapse.

Conclusion

In this chapter, we have covered a range of more advanced approaches to posting on Instagram. However, this is not an exhaustive list. Continue to expand your knowledge of these new posting approaches. New apps, services, and techniques are developed all the time. Instagram, remember, is a product of technology. As technology continues, you must adapt to it in order to stay relevant and ahead of the curve.

PART 3: MONETIZATION & MARKETING

CHAPTER 6: HOW TO MAKE MONEY ON INSTAGRAM

In this chapter, we are going to explore how you can fully monetize your Instagram account. For many who take their Instagram profile seriously, this is the end goal. If you are an individual person using yourself as your brand, then using Instagram logically leads to you being able to make a good living from your Instagram posts. Likewise, if you are using your Instagram account as promotion for a business or product, you want Instagram to lead directly into sales and other financial opportunities.

With this in mind, let us look then at some of the best ways to make money on Instagram.

Merchandize

Selling merchandize on your Instagram account is a no-brainer. Your own personal merchandize is intimately connected to your brand. It should carry your brand message and style with it. This is the key difference between what is considered merchandize and what is considered an outright product. A product can be used for a specific task, like a blender or car. Merchandize, on the other hand, has been made for one purpose. It carries your brand message with it. Think of someone wearing a T-shirt with their favourite band logo on it. Another example would be a baseball cap with sports team branding on it. Of course, there are places where merchandize and products kind of become the same thing and overlap. For example, Nike produces trainers. People wear those trainers, and those trainers contain the logo for Nike on them for all to see. So in that case, the trainers kind of become both merchandize and a product to be used.

Here are a few merchandising ideas for you to consider for your Instagram account:

1. **T-shirts**

2. **Posters**

3. **Calendars**

4. **Keychains**

5. **Stickers**

6. **Patches**

7. **Pins**

8. **Clothes**

9. **Hats**

10. **Cups**

11. **Bags**

What all these examples have in common is that merchandize carries with it a focus on your brand.

Think of it as a win-win situation. If one of your followers buys some merchandize and then wears and displays it, you get some free advertising into the bargain. What is great about merchandising is that if you are not able to make these items in-house, there are a number of great third-party services such as Teespring which will allow you to quickly produce T-shirts and other items en masse and on demand for your Instagram followers. You can then promote these items via your Instagram account and other social media profiles.

Sell Your Images

Instagram is a visual medium, and so photographs and other images are incredibly important. But they can also be a source of income for an Instagram user. Perhaps you have taken a fantastic picture of an animal in its natural habitat or maybe you have had a photo shoot organized and uploaded. Another example would be capturing an incredible moment incidentally. Whatever it is, these images can be sold.

Options for selling your images include:

1. Uploading for use as stock images via sites such as Shutterstock.

2. Selling your images for use in the press via newspapers, magazines, and news websites.

3. Licence your image for use on promotional materials.

4. Upload your image for use via online printers where people can create their own

bespoke posters, cushions, clothes, and other items.

5. You can also sell your Instagram images directly on websites like Twenty20.

Whenever you do use an image, ensure that you include a disclaimer or contract covering exactly where the image is allowed to be used. This will protect you from the plethora of people and businesses who want to use material for free.

Affiliate Marketing & Sponsored Posts

With affiliate marketing, you make money every time one of your followers clicks a link to check out a product or buy it. With a sponsored post, you are directly paid by a company to promote or review a product. Both can be used to generate significant revenues. Affiliate marketing through companies like Amazon allow you to place a URL (which might not be clickable, which we will discuss later) in your sidebar to a product without even having an agreement specifically with the manufacturer in place. You will then be paid a percentage of the sales from the people who follow that link.

Often as your Instagram page grows, companies will approach you to promote their goods in return for money, a free product, or a discount on something else they are offering. It is down to you to negotiate the terms of these deals. However, you can seek such deals yourself and be partnered with a sponsor through websites such as Sharesale, Ebates, and Stylinity.

Sell a Product or Service

This is going to be especially important for those who are running their Instagram account as part of a business. Selling your products or services through Instagram is a great way to reach new paying customers. You can promote your products by sharing behind-the-scenes information and customer photos. You can also run discounts and other giveaways to increase goodwill towards your brand.

It is a good idea to include a direct link to your product in your profile bio via the website link, and to also include them in your promotional posts where allowed. You can also reach agreements with other Instagram users to promote your services and products. You can do this either by reaching a sponsorship agreement or providing a free product/service for review.

Sell Your Instagram Account

Lastly, you can actually sell your Instagram account. If you build up significant following, you will be able to sell your Instagram brand/account to a third party who will then have access to your followers. You can then walk away to other ventures. An alternative to this, is to sell your account with an agreement that you will still be involved in some capacity as a creative consultant or shareholder.

Believe it or not, there are services which will help you find a buyer for your Instagram account.

Websites such as Fame Swap and Viral Accounts are just two options for those looking to sell or buy Instagram accounts. For some, this is the end goal of their Instagram account; for others they will sell their Instagram account once they feel their brand is in decline. They will then set up a new Instagram account under a new brand and start all over again, but with a substantial amount of money in the bank from the sale of their original Instagram account.

Conclusion

In this chapter, we have covered ways in which you can monetize your Instagram account. Other creative options for monetization do exist, but the above recommendations tend to cover the majority of monetization strategies. By following one of these or a combination of them, it is possible to not only make a living from Instagram, but to also make financial gains well beyond this.

Chapter 7: The Secret to Successful Ads and Promotions

In this chapter, we are going to cover the best ways to get the most out of ads and promotions on Instagram. These apply to both promoting yourself and being sponsored. Results will vary, but if you follow the steps taken in this chapter, you will maximize the amount of revenue you can make from ads and promotions, while extending your brand reach.

Linking in Instagram

Whether you are posting about your products or a sponsored product/service, most advertisers will want you to put a link to their products in the description of a post. Unfortunately, at the time of this writing, this can be difficult on Instagram. A quirk of Instagram is that you cannot post *clickable* links in your organic post descriptions unless you have a special type of account. You can, however, post them in your bio as your single website link. But then, why have we mentioned posting links in your sidebar throughout this book? The reason is that there is a difference between:

1. **Standard Instagram posts**
2. **Verified Posts**

In a **standard post**, you cannot include such links in a clickable form, only text. If you have a **verified account**, then you will be able to post such links which can then be clicked. To become verified, however, you will have to have a substantial following. Alternatively, you need to have a business profile as opposed to a personal account and have more than 10,000 followers.

But what about the mere mortals who do not have the ability to get verified yet? Well, there are a few workarounds:

1. **Captions**: Include the link in the caption to your photo or image. It will not be clickable, but your users will be   able   to copy the link and paste it into their browser.

2. **Another Account**: You can set up another Instagram account through a disposable email address and then include the link you want in the new account's profile. When you post your image or video, you can then put the name of that account in the post. It will be clickable. People will click on it and will be taken to the profile of that other account. It is messy, but will get people to the link you want them to click.

With these workarounds in place, you will be able to more successfully place affiliate links and links to your own adverts through your content.

Secrets to Running Effective Ads

If you are going to run your own adverts and promote your own products/merchandize, then it is essential that you understand some basic advertising techniques which will boost your effectiveness. You can also apply these to offering a better advertising strategy to third parties as well, if they do not provide you with specific advertising guidelines.

These include:

1. Having a clear message.

2. Having a concise message which is easily understood without your audience having to jump through any hoops.

3. Having a branded message which can be instantly connected to you and your products.

4. Targeting your audience demographic through paid ads.

5. Designing your adverts with a demographic in mind, stylistically creating something which will resonate with them on both an aesthetic and symbolic level.

6. Create adverts which are captivating visually.

7. Do not over saturate with repeat postings.

8. Listen to audience feedback.

How to Promote Successfully

Promoting something via affiliate marketing or sponsorship on Instagram requires a bespoke approach which is appropriate to the product, service, or individual you are marketing. However, there are some specific lessons which can be applied to promotion on Instagram, which will increase the likelihood that your approach will be successful.

When formulating your plan, keep the following in mind:

- **Positive Association**: Psychology plays a huge part in any type of advertising. If an advertiser has contacted you and asked you to promote their product or service, they understand that already. It is down to you to take advantage of this psychological aspect and be persuasive. Positive Association is a huge part of this. Try to present the positive side of what you are promoting. Your followers will only buy a product if associated with a positive experience. Keep your criticisms then to a minimum.

- **High Energy**: As well as being positive about a promoted item, you should try and remain high-energy when presenting it. The 18 to 35-year-old demographic which most advertisers are interested in, implicitly expects enthusiasm about the product. You can be as positive about a product as possible, but if you present that in a low-energy way, people will not be interested in what you have to say.

- **Captivate:** The advertising you make for a product or service needs to be captivating.

There are two aspects to being captivating. The first is to catch the eye and the second is to hold the attention. Think about these two things when designing your approach. You want something that followers are going to be immediately interested in, but you want to present it in such a way that they will not get bored.

- **Engage:** Lastly, if you are unable to engage your audience then advertiser paid promotions will surely dry up. Advertisers want to see a real return on the paid posts you have provided. Engagement is the way to make sure that the promotions you run, work. And by engagement, we are talking about your followers taking an action in some capacity like the CTAs we mentioned earlier. This could be with a comment or a like. Ideally, it will be following a link to a paid product and then making a purchasing decision. When advertisers see that you are able to persuade your followers to purchase goods in this way, many more of them will come forward with promotional opportunities. Think about engagement, think about funneling your followers towards buying a product. If this is at the core of your approach, any advertising promotion will be successful. This applies to promoting both your own brand and the products/services of a third party.

Be Wary

Be very wary when entering into advertising. Your brand is a lasting thing, and to ensure its success you have to be trusted. This is true of Instagram more than any other platform on the planet. The connection between you and your followers means something. If your followers feel that you have betrayed their trust, they will abandon you swiftly. In other words, do not promote a product which is extremely flawed at best, or worst, is seen as some sort of misleading scam. It does not matter how much money you are offered, your brand and your success in the future demands that you promote ethically to your followers. To avoid these problems, ask to try out any service or product that you are promoting. Get used to it, and think about how others will react when they buy that product/service.

Conclusion

In this chapter, we have covered the secrets behind running successful ads and promotions. These can be applied to your own promotions and sponsored deals. Stay ethical, stay positive, at all times keep your eyes open when promoting. If you do that and drive your followers towards engagement, you will continue to be successful both as an Instagram user and a promoter of third-party goods.

If you're enjoying this book, I would appreciate it if you went to the place of purchase and left a short positive review. Thank you

PART 4: BE INSPIRED

CHAPTER 8: THE MINDSET OF AN INSTAGRAM STAR

N ow that you have a great idea of how to run a successful Instagram account and how to grow it, the one final ingredient is mindset. Why are some Instagram users successful and yet others are not? Is it the case that some people just have talent and others do not? Are those of us who do not have success damned to accept failure? Of course not! The difference between a successful Instagram user and an unsuccessful one can be boiled down to having the **right mindset**. In this chapter we are going to briefly look at the type of mindset you need to become an Instagram star.

Looking at all of the successful Instagram users, you will see traits which are shared between them all. Sure, there will be the odd person who has simply found success through sheer luck. But, the majority of Instagram users who are successful, have done so by relying on, or cultivating, certain approaches to success. These can be boiled down to four main characteristics:

1. **Passion**
2. **Discipline**
3. **Hard Work**

4. Study

We will now look at each of these. As you read about them, be honest about yourself. Which characteristics do you possess? And if you do not possess one or more of these, do not feel downhearted, instead persevere and move forward to cultivate these characteristics within yourself.

Passion

To be a success and to combine this with longevity requires passion. A drive towards something which you truly care about. It is contagious to be around someone who is filled with passion for what they are doing. It is one of the reasons why people watch Instagram users and Youtubers. That level of passion is infectious and makes us feel more alive. But it does more than that when you are an Instagram user. Passion is what gets you through difficult times. When things are not quite going your way, it is passion which provides you with comfort. There is still an enjoyment in what you are doing. A love for it. If you have a love for the brand, product/service, or idea you are trying to convey through Instagram, then nothing can stand in your way. You will attract people to you because passion is addictive. It pushes on and gives us the energy to achieve, and it is something that people like to be around.

Discipline

But despite the passion which we may have, it is discipline which truly makes us endure. You will often hear people talking about trying to find inspiration. Or rather, they will wait for it to appear. Writers often talk about having writer's block. However, it is not true that you have to wait to push through these times. What you truly require is discipline. The ability to sit down regularly and get the work done. Discipline is what gives us the ability to organize and plan. These are two critical talents when creating an Instagram account which will resonate with people. Content plans do not just appear out of the ether. When we do not feel like working, it is discipline which tells us we *must*. It is discipline which gets us to at least start and try when we feel tired. And so cultivate discipline, you will find that every successful Instagram user who posts consistently, does so because discipline gets them through when they cannot be bothered to post.

Hard Work

Attached to discipline is the idea of hard work. Instagram users often look as though they are effortlessly living and producing first-class content. But this is not true. It is hard work which produces results. If you think being an Instagram user is not going to be difficult or does not require effort, then you will fail. Being an Instagram star is not about avoiding work, it is about embracing work which we need to do in order to make things happen.

Work which enriches our lives both financially and emotionally. Be prepared to work hard. Roll up your sleeves and get stuck into your content plan. With hard work, you will scale the mountain. Without it, you will continue to look up at the peak and wonder what could have been.

Study

Finally, study is an essential part of the Instagram star mindset. All the people who are successful on Instagram stay abridged of technological changes and trends which they must be aware of. The last thing you want for your brand is to appear irrelevant and out of touch. And so, you must continue to study new ways to market yourself; along with what your competitors are doing, new changes being made to Instagram as a service, and any new applications which may make your profile more successful. Always be a student. Always learn. And always take this new knowledge forward with you, using it in a way which is innovative and inspirational.

Conclusion

In this chapter, we have covered the four main aspects of the winning Instagram mentality. The mentality which separates those who are successful on Instagram from those who are unsuccessful. As I mentioned at the beginning of this chapter, if you feel you are lacking in any of these four areas, then take that as a positive thing. Use it as an opportunity to open yourself up to learn more. Drive yourself forward with the commitment that you are going to take on these mindsets. At first, it will be difficult. All habits are. But after just a few weeks, you will notice a huge change in who you are. You will have gone from someone who is lost, to someone who is passionately and purposefully moving towards an achievable goal. The goal of being a true Instagram star.

Chapter 9: Inspirational Instagram Success Stories

In this chapter, we are going to look at inspirational success stories. These are success stories which you can turn to in times when things are perhaps not going your way. Remember that all the people who have had successes on Instagram at one time were failing. The following three inspirational accounts are there to show you that being a success on Instagram, more than anything else, is about staying the course.

An Eye For Success

In 2013, Chris Buckard had not yet experienced success as a photographer. At least, he had not reached his potential. It was Instagram which provided this potential. At that time, he was travelling, trying to make his living photographing the world around him. But when he was introduced to Instagram by a friend, his world eventually changed. He started out humbly, sharing the photographs which he had taken on his travels. It took some time to gain traction, but that decision to start sharing photographs on Instagram changed Chris Buckard's life forever. At the time of this writing, he has over 3.4 million followers on Instagram. It has become a bit of a career in of itself. His secret was people valued the content he was producing - the beautiful photographs which captured the incredible vistas and amazing moments for his followers to enjoy. Because he maintained that same dedication to quality, his posts resonated with people. That in turn, brought in an audience. Remember this, when things are not going according to plan. Brilliant success may be just around the corner, and you are not even aware of it.

Dressed to Thrill

Anish Bhatt is one of the most inspirational people on Instagram. At the time of this writing, he has around 1.7 million followers. But he was not always that successful. In his late 20s, Anish was facing personal ruin. He had been fired from his job and the road ahead was dark and uncertain. He was forced to abandon the life he had tried to make for himself and head back home to his parents. But what he did next, changed his life forever. Anish leveraged the talents he had. He had learned a lot about fashion design and photography. He then combined this with his passion for watches, and began taking stunning pictures related to this, sharing them on Instagram. While advertising is important, it costs money. This is something Anish did not have. It is incredible that he reached well over 1 million fans in a purely organic way without ever paying for an advert. He was interested in other Instagram users and their passions. He connected with people, he engaged with those around him on Instagram. And then he put himself at the centre of his brand. Now, instead of marketing watches and fashion, he markets himself. This has taken him to Monaco, London, and Dubai. He is a true jet setter, and it is all thanks to Instagram. His dreams were made possible because they grew out of the ruins of his previous life. Social media can do that, it can turn the darkest moments of our lives into stories of joy and abundance.

A Good Mood

Many turn to Instagram for motivational help. Jason Stone is one of the most successful people who has harnessed this area within Instagram. By using his Instagram account to convey positive thinking and inspirational moments, the world has been captivated by his account. Not only that, but what started out as a drive of passion has quickly turned into a lucrative business with numerous passive revenue streams. Generating more than a hundred thousand dollars a month, he does this without investing in any advertising. But what Jason did next, should prove even more inspirational to entrepreneurs. He took one type of Instagram account and then used it to open up another door in his life. He created a business which offers low-cost advertising to smaller businesses. He generated the momentum to build that business into a huge franchize with millions of dollars. The business, known as Door Coupons, has expanded to many countries across the globe already. It continues to grow and is an excellent example of how one person can use their personality and positivity to then monetize their content through business investment. Jason Stone is just one individual who has achieved this, but there are many more. If you are hoping to break out into many different business fields and beyond, then this is one story which is worth holding onto as a guide.

Conclusion

The point of these stories is to motivate you. It is to help you see that people do not always start with success. What Instagram offers more than anything else is beautiful uncertainty. The success which comes with Instagram opens new doors. It channels your energies into unseen, unpredictable positive avenues. Just by posting images and videos on the Internet, you are able to generate, not just an income, but an entire way of life which will positively affect all your loved ones and even millions of strangers around the globe. Return to these stories and study other success stories as you encounter them. There are things to be learned there, and in your darker times when things are not quite going your way, you will feel motivated by the fact that these successful people were once in your exact circumstances, and then prevailed.

AFTERWORD

This book is only the beginning of your Instagram journey. It is a blueprint to a better future. A way to reach your goals. Build on what you have learned through these chapters. Continue to be a student of **trends** and **innovation**. Cultivate the correct approach of the **Instagram star mindset**. Continue along your journey and never be afraid to alter your approach when things are not working as you had hoped. Instagram is a competitive place, but if you **leverage your individuality** in everything you do, then you will have a great chance at success. Because Instagram is about celebrating individuality of people, products, and businesses. By celebrating your uniqueness, you can give something to the world that no one else can - **you**.

If you enjoyed this book, I would appreciate it if you went to the place of purchase and left a short positive review. Thank you